Beyond Diagnosis

Reclaiming the Neurodivergent Self Through Reflection, Care, and Accommodation

Danna Bodenheimer

Contents

Introduction

Let us begin with the understanding that it is exhausting to debate definitions or criteria for autism when there is no clear or definitive answer. Yet this is the position many of us find ourselves in when we try to understand our own minds. Autism is not confirmed by a blood test. There is no single threshold, no universally agreed-upon presentation, no diagnostic measure that can fully capture lived experience. And still, people are asked—often urgently—to make sense of themselves within systems that demand certainty.

You may have considered pursuing a formal diagnosis for autism and/or ADHD. You may already have one. Or you may have found the diagnostic process inaccessible, inconclusive, or actively harmful. Handing over interpretive authority about your inner life to a practitioner who is not neuro-affirming can leave lasting psychological scars. Handing over thousands of dollars for an assessment that still fails to see you clearly can leave a different kind of mark. For many, the diagnostic pathway does not bring clarity—it brings confusion, invalidation, or silence.

This workbook was created for those of us who have spent years feeling out of step with the world, for those who noticed early on that certain environments, expectations, or relationships felt unbearable. In contrast, others seemed to move through them with ease. It is for people who adapted by masking, compensating, and performing functionality so thoroughly that internal signals became faint at best and inaudible at worst.

This book is for clinicians, for curious thinkers, and for people seeking a deeper understanding of how their minds work. It is for those who have been told—explicitly or implicitly—that they are too much, too sensitive, too analytical, too inconsistent, or somehow misaligned with the pace and demands of the world around them.

Rather than asking you to arrive at a conclusion about who you are, this workbook invites you into a process of self-exploration. For many autistic people, understanding our neurotype—and other neurodivergent people—whether formally named or not—has been essential to survival. It has allowed for the creation of accommodations, boundaries, and life structures that reduce chronic shutdown, burnout, and self-erasure. At the same time, this process is not simple. It asks you to trust your own perceptions in a culture that has repeatedly taught you not to.

Professional diagnosis relies on assessment tools that are historically skewed toward white, upper- to middle-class populations, most of whom are male. These evaluations often combine self-report, third-party observations, and clinician interpretation of observable behaviors against criteria outlined in the DSM-5. What they frequently fail to capture is internal experience: sensory overwhelm, cognitive fatigue, pattern recognition, emotional processing, and the cost of constant adaptation.

The irony is that many autistic people have been trained—often from a very young age—to mask precisely the traits clinicians are looking for. Research has shown that masking can render autistic experience invisible to external observers while increasing internal distress (Miller et al., 2021). Much of autistic life happens internally, beyond language, beyond performance, beyond what is easily measured. These internal processes are complex, nuanced, and often hidden to survive within systems shaped by ableism.

That is where this book comes in.

Just as formal diagnostic systems are limited, so is this workbook. There is nothing official about it. What it offers instead is space. Space to reflect on how autistic ways of being may have shaped your past. Space to understand your current patterns, capacities, and struggles. Space to imagine a future that is not organized around fixing yourself, but around understanding what you need to live with greater safety, coherence, and self-respect.

What This Workbook Offers

This workbook provides a wide range of information about autism, including the many ways autistic traits can manifest across a lifetime. This information is not offered as a checklist or a test. It is offered as context—something to think alongside as you reflect on your own experiences.

Please consider this book an ally. It holds knowledge, but not authority over your inner life. It is interactive and reflective, offering space for writing, noticing, questioning, and meaning-making. Throughout this process, you are invited to remain the primary interpreter of your own experience.

To be clear from the outset, this guidebook is rooted in politics. By "politics," I mean it explicitly examines how power operates in mental healthcare, diagnosis, and treatment. This book questions the ways autism has been medicalized, monetized, and managed within systems shaped by capitalism, white supremacy, heteronormativity, cisnormativity, and ableism.

The term *autism industrial complex* refers to the network of institutions, organizations, professionals, and industries that have emerged around autism—including research, diagnosis, treatment, education, and advocacy. These systems often rely economically on the continued pathologization of autistic bodies and experiences.

Researcher Anne McGuire (2016) describes it this way:

> *The body of the autistic child has generated a multibillion-dollar "autism industrial complex"—public and private investment interests that benefit economically from, and indeed whose very fiscal survival is reliant upon, the existence of autistic bodies (p. 126).*

The intention behind this workbook is not to replace one authority with another. It is to protect autistic people from frameworks that fragment identity, undermine self-trust, and disconnect individuals from their own histories and needs.

There is space for you here. While there are many words, there are also pages designed for your own reflections. This workbook is a co-creation between you and the text. Its purpose is to center your experience, support self-advocacy, and help you identify accommodations that allow you to remain intact.

As you move through these pages, you may begin to notice patterns—not as problems to eliminate, but as information. Each prompt is an invitation to explore what has protected you, what it has cost you, and what might finally feel safe enough to soften or unmask.

You do not need to complete this workbook in order or all at once. You can skip sections, return later, or pause entirely. Choosing how and when you engage is part of attunement.

This is not a workbook that tries to fix you. It assumes you already hold knowledge about yourself—and that this knowledge deserves time, care, and respect.

Reflection

After reading this introduction, take a moment to write about your internal response.

1. What feelings arise as you consider exploring autism through reflection rather than proof?

2. What fears, hopes, or resistances do you notice?

3. Can you allow yourself to remain in process, without forcing clarity or certainty?

4. Regardless of where you land, how might this exploration shape the way you understand yourself and others?

Who Danna Is, and Why This Perspective Matters

I bring over twenty years of healthcare experience to this work. Over that time, I have come to see both the immense harm and the profound limitations embedded in how our systems understand autism, mental health, and difference more broadly. I am also acutely aware of how politically and socially distorted these frameworks can be— and how urgently they need to be reimagined. Re-humanizing neurodivergent people is not optional; it is necessary.

Loneliness is a common thread in the autistic experience. I understand that loneliness intimately.

For much of my life, I have felt like an iceberg—what is visible above the surface rarely reflects the vastness beneath it. What I show the world and what I experience internally have often felt misaligned. And while that can be isolating, I want you to know this: you are not alone in the effort to feel more integrated.

I want to begin by sharing a few ways I experience the world.

From childhood, I have been intensely sensitive to certain sensory environments. Milk—particularly skim milk—has always been unbearable for me to be around. Kitchens, too, can feel chaotic and overwhelming, places of concentrated sensory overload that I instinctively avoid. These are not preferences so much as nervous system responses.

Emotionally, my inner life has its own distinct rhythm. I can name emotions with precision, yet I do not always feel them linearly or immediately. My thoughts tend to arrive first; feelings follow later, often on their own unpredictable timeline. I do not experience myself as especially direct. Much of what I hold goes unspoken—not because it is unimportant, but because staying engaged in the ways expected of me often requires restraint.

Others sometimes perceive me as blunt or overly direct. What they may not see is the amount of effort it takes for me to arrive at words at all. Icebergs, after all, are likely lonely. They are also melting. And while I am not equating unmasking with global catastrophe—one must happen, the other must end—I am saying this: the conditions that once allowed me to hide no longer exist. My nervous system will not allow it. This realization has been painful. It has also been liberating.

I have an unusually detail-oriented memory and a deep love of collecting information. This trait has been alternately mocked and rewarded throughout my life. I now understand it as both a form of hypervigilance and a genuine source of pleasure. I love to study, to catalog, to know. Sometimes I joke that I would have worked for the FBI if I weren't a therapist—until I remember that I struggle deeply with institutions and social constructs that demand performance over integrity.

Relationships can feel maddening to navigate. I am deeply grateful for spaces—particularly therapeutic ones—where there is room to speak honestly, without small talk or performative ease. The therapy room has often felt euphorically relieving to me precisely because its boundaries are fluid and explicit. Outside of those spaces, I frequently feel misread: too intense, too direct, uninterested in niceties unless they intersect with something I genuinely care about.

My relationship to gender has also resisted easy categorization. I do not experience femininity or masculinity as accessible scripts. Over time, I have come to understand my gender through neurodivergent frameworks—sometimes described as neuroqueer or auti-gender—not as an identity to perform, but as an acknowledgment that binary social constructs do not translate cleanly through my cognitive processes or nervous system. I do not have the script. I also cannot tolerate pants that feel constricting.

At different times in my life, I have lived with panic, depression, body dysmorphia, gender dysphoria, and pervasive anxiety. For years, these experiences were treated as separate issues—symptoms to be managed rather than signals to be understood. Autism was never meaningfully considered. According to prevailing frameworks, I did not "look" autistic. I was deemed too high-functioning.

It was only later—through reflection, study, and listening deeply to both my clients and myself—that an autistic lens began to bring coherence to experiences that once felt fragmented. Viewing my life through this framework did not provide certainty. It provided understanding. And with that understanding came relief, grief, and a reorganization of how I relate to myself and the world.

Throughout my academic training, including the completion of a doctoral degree, autism was notably absent. I learned about ethics, mandated reporting, and student loan debt—but not neurodiversity. Not once. This absence continued throughout my post-graduate education. The few trainings

I did encounter often dehumanized neurodivergent people rather than honoring their lived realities.

My early clinical work focused on LGBTQ+ communities through lenses of affirmation and de-pathologization. Over time, my clients became my greatest teachers. They revealed to me the deep intersections between autism and queerness, between identity and nervous system, between adaptation and survival. As my understanding has grown, so has my tolerance for not knowing. Certainty has become less important than curiosity, care, and humility.

Regarding Autism

Many autistic people experience social confusion early in life—on playgrounds, in classrooms, at dinner tables. There can be pressure to eat foods that cause genuine distress, to tolerate overwhelming environments, or to endure the exhaustion of being either overstimulated or under-stimulated. Burnout often follows.

Traits such as introversion and extroversion exist independently of autism, despite common misconceptions. What is often overlooked is the sensitivity and depth of the autistic nervous system: the capacity for wonder, the intensity of special interests, and the profound connection many autistic people feel to what they love.

Autistic individuals are frequently presumed to lack insight into themselves or into what would alleviate their distress. My experience—and my clinical work—suggests otherwise.

Reclaiming joy and special interests

As we come to understand our neurotype, joy can take on new meaning. Many autistic minds are wired to study, to savor, and to dive deeply into areas of fascination. These interests are not indulgences. They are sources of regulation, connection, and vitality.

Reflection

1.   What subjects, patterns, or activities could you spend endless time exploring?

2.   When was the last time you felt fully absorbed in something, without self-consciousness?

3.   How might you create more room for that kind of joy in your current life?

Your special interests are not distractions from life. They are central to it.

Takeaway

This book is not just about me. It is about making room for you.

I share my experience not as a template, but as an opening. The language in this workbook is intentionally spacious—designed to hold both painful and liberating truths. I believe that reducing performativity, questioning harmful norms, and honoring deep integrity are not only acts of self-preservation but acts of collective care.

Spend time with this book alongside your history, your inner life, and your hopes. Give yourself permission to uncover the parts of you that were taught to stay hidden. Whether this process remains private or becomes shared, it belongs to you.

It is your turn.

Reflection

Now that you know a bit about me and why I wrote this book, I invite you to turn inward.

1. What personal characteristics have made you wonder if you experience the world differently?

2. What drew you to this book at this moment?

3. Which ideas resonated with you—and which felt uncomfortable or contentious?

Unmasking is only part of the story.

For many people, unmasking is described as a moment of clarity or relief. But clarity alone does not create safety. Once you begin to recognize what overwhelms you, what drains you, and what you have been compensating for, the next question becomes: *What will support me now?*

Self-exploration without protection can be destabilizing. Awareness without accommodation can leave you more exposed than before. This is why the work of understanding yourself must be paired with the work of building structures that can actually sustain you—at work, at home, and in relationships.

The structures in your life are already shaping your nervous system, whether intentionally or not. Schedules, expectations, sensory environments, relational dynamics, productivity demands—these forces either help regulate you or quietly exhaust you. This chapter invites you to notice where your current structures require you to perform, tolerate, or override yourself to function.

Protection does not mean avoidance or shrinking your life. It means designing systems that account for fluctuation. Many neurodivergent people experience energy, attention, emotion, and sensory tolerance as variable rather than consistent. A structure that only works on your "best" days is not sustainable. Flexibility is not a failure of discipline; it is an act of realism.

Self-exploration, in this context, is not about searching for deficits. It is about gathering information. You are learning how your nervous system responds to time, space, sound, pace, relational proximity, and demand. This information can guide decisions about boundaries, routines, and accommodations— not because you are fragile, but because you are specific.

The goal is not to eliminate distress entirely. That is neither possible nor necessary. The goal is to reduce unnecessary harm. To create enough predictability, choice, and recovery that overwhelm does not become the organizing principle of your life.

As you move through this chapter, you may notice resistance. You may have learned that needing support is weakness, that asking for accommodation is indulgent, or that pushing through is the only respectable option. Those beliefs did not come from nowhere, but they do not have to dictate how you care for yourself now.

The work here is subtle. It happens in small decisions: how you structure your day, where you expend energy, what you stop apologizing for, and what you allow yourself to need.

Reflection

In earlier sections, we explored the concept of masking—how and why people learn to conceal parts of themselvestoo remain safe, functional, or accepted. Use the questions below to begin connecting awareness with protection.

1. Can you identify situations in which you tend to put on a mask?

2. How does masking affect you physically, emotionally, or cognitively—during the moment and afterward?

3. How do you feel in environments where you do not experience pressure to mask?

4. What routines, systems, or ways of organizing your life actually work for you—even if they seem unconventional or misunderstood by others?

5. What supports (tools, people, spaces, practices) help your life feel more easeful or regulated?

6. Knowing that overwhelm and distress are sometimes inevitable responses to environmental demands, how might you build flexibility—rather than rigidity—into your structures?

You are not being asked to implement changes all at once. Noticing is enough. Protection often begins with permission.

Those of us who identify with autism are not unified by a single presentation. No two autistic people share the same exact traits, expressions, or capacities. This variability is one reason diagnostic criteria often feel insufficient or imprecise. At the same time, shared themes connect the autistic experience and enable collective understanding.

Two broad cornerstones are commonly present. The first involves how the brain processes, stores, and communicates information. The second involves a nervous system that differs from what is considered neuro-normative. This nervous system may be more or less sensitive, or uneven in its response to the world. These differences are not inherently pathological. Much of what becomes disruptive in autistic lives emerges not from autism itself, but from chronic exposure to environments that do not accommodate neurological difference.

Autism has historically been described as a neurodevelopmental disorder—something measured in terms of delay, deficit, or deviation from a presumed norm. It has often been evaluated through behaviors such as social difficulty, repetitive actions, or differences in communication. This workbook does not adopt that framework. Autism is not explored here through the lenses of deficiency or failed development.

A "delay" assumes there is a universal timeline for growth. There is not. A "deficit" implies something is missing from the autistic mind. This assumption is symbolized clearly in the puzzle-piece imagery that has long dominated autism-related advocacy and fundraising. Entire industries have been built around locating autism's causes, detecting it earlier, and correcting it faster. Alongside this, shame has quietly permeated cultural narratives—shame about difference, about needing support, about failing to perform neuro-normativity convincingly enough.

This book rejects hierarchies of social understanding. Autistic people do not lack awareness of social cues; instead, they may be attuned to different ones. Just because someone does not respond in line with dominant expectations does not mean those expectations go unnoticed. Many autistic individuals expend enormous energy tracking, decoding, and compensating for social norms—even when those norms do not feel intuitive or meaningful.

One way to understand autism is as a particular way of perceiving and organizing the world. Autistic minds are often drawn toward depth: deep research, deep focus, deep expertise, deep care. Contrary to outdated stereotypes, autistic people are not deficient in empathy. Many experience empathy intensely—sometimes overwhelmingly. This heightened empathic attunement can contribute to emotional and sensory overload, eventually leading to shutdown rather than disengagement.

The autistic nervous system itself can be highly sensitive, though sensitivity does not look the same for everyone. Sounds that fade into the background for some may register as blaring or invasive. Foods that seem neutral to others may cause sensory overwhelm. Some autistic people feel regulated by high levels of sensory input, such as weighted blankets, layered textures, constant sound, and visual stimulation. Others require minimal sensory input to remain grounded and rely on quiet, predictable foods or controlled environments. Many people fluctuate between these needs depending on stress, fatigue, and context.

There is no correct sensory profile. There is only information.

Regardless of how autism shows up in your life, this workbook makes room for it. The goal is not to compare your experience to anyone else's or to assess whether it qualifies. The goal is to help you articulate the shape of your own nervous system, your processing style, your sensory needs, and your pathways to regulation.

Understanding autism in this way is not about labeling. It is about orientation. It offers language where there may have been only confusion, and context where there may have been only self-blame.

Reflection

Rather than moving toward certainty, use the questions below to explore resonance.

1. Which descriptions in this chapter felt familiar or relieving?

2. Where did you notice resistance, discomfort, or skepticism?

3. How would your life change if your sensory and processing needs were treated as information rather than problems?

4. What environments tend to support your regulation—and which quietly deplete you?

You are not being asked to decide anything here. You are being invited to notice.

Chapter 3
About Diagnosis

Diagnosis is often treated as a finish line—a moment of clarity that resolves uncertainty and confers legitimacy. In reality, diagnosis is a system: shaped by economics, power, culture, and access. For some people, a formal diagnosis is affirming and useful. For others, it is confusing, unavailable, or actively harmful. This chapter is not about persuading you toward or away from a diagnosis. It is about helping you understand what a diagnosis can and cannot do.

What is a formal diagnosis?

A formal autism diagnosis is typically made through a comprehensive evaluation conducted by a licensed psychologist trained in neuropsychological assessment. Psychiatrists may also diagnose autism, though they do not usually administer the same extensive testing batteries. These evaluations attempt to determine whether a person's experiences and behaviors align with current diagnostic frameworks.

It is common for impostor syndrome to surface during this process. Much of the information required—particularly for adults—relies on self-report, memory, and interpretation. There is no blood test, brain scan, or definitive biological marker for autism. Outcomes vary. Some people receive a diagnosis that feels resonant and relieving. Others leave with inconclusive results or outright dismissal, which can destabilize an emerging sense of self-understanding.

How the diagnostic process works

The formal diagnostic process often includes several stages:

Initial screening

A general practitioner or mental health provider may determine whether further evaluation is warranted. This is where much of the gatekeeping around autism occurs. Access to diagnosis often hinges on whether someone else perceives your experience as "concerning enough."

Comprehensive assessment

Children are often assessed by multidisciplinary teams. Adults are typically evaluated by a single psychologist, who may request input from family members or others who know you well. For many adults, this corroboration is unavailable—sometimes a limitation, sometimes a relief, given how subjective and biased external reports can be.

Interviews and observation

Developmental history, communication style, and social interaction are evaluated. For children, caregiver reports carry significant weight. For adults, the absence of early documentation can complicate assessment, even when lived experience is clear.

Standardized measures

Diagnostic tools rely heavily on observable behaviors and assumptions about social norms. These tools were largely developed based on white, cisgender, neurotypical/allistic populations. They do not reliably account for masking, cultural differences, gender diversity, or internal experience. One should be aware that these tools may not have been designed with them in mind.

Diagnostic determination

Using the collected data, the evaluator determines whether the criteria outlined in diagnostic manuals such as the DSM-5 are met. Adults often lack access to many of the data points used to justify certainty, making diagnostic conclusions, at best, uneven.

Benefits and limitations of diagnosis

A formal diagnosis can provide access to accommodations, workplace protections, educational support, and government benefits. It can reduce the need to repeatedly explain yourself to providers and systems. For some families, it legitimizes experience and fosters understanding.

At the same time, diagnosis has limitations. Accommodations are enforceable only in environments governed by laws such as the ADA. Bureaucratic systems may support or hinder autistic people depending on their rigidity. Diagnosis can also become reductive—used to explain away complexity or constrain identity.

Some people experience increased stigma following diagnosis. Others experience relief. Some feel both. Validation is not guaranteed, and credibility can be unevenly granted depending on race, gender, age, and presentation.

Diagnosis is not neutral. It is a tool, and like all tools, it works better in some hands than others.

Beyond diagnosis

Many people come to understand themselves not through diagnosis, but through lived experience, reflection, and pattern recognition. Autism is not always discovered through testing. Often, it emerges through exhaustion, resonance, and the slow realization that familiar struggles share a common thread.

Much of the autistic experience is internal: sensory processing, pattern recognition, empathy, and cognitive load. These realities are frequently invisible to evaluators—especially when masking is present. Many autistic people learn early that showing themselves honestly results in rejection, misunderstanding, or harm.

Understanding yourself through this lens is not about certainty. It is about coherence.

Why understanding yourself matters

Self-knowledge shapes protection. When you understand how your nervous system responds to sound, demand, social pressure, or unpredictability, you are better equipped to advocate for yourself—formally or informally.

Consider misophonia. If you understand your response to gum chewing as a nervous system reaction rather than personal irritability, you can set boundaries with less shame. The same is true for sensory overwhelm, fatigue, or social exhaustion. Language changes response. Understanding creates possibility.

Everyone has a neurotype. When people live in alignment with their realities—rather than against them—they reduce unnecessary suffering.

The grief of recognition

Understanding yourself through a neurodivergent lens often brings grief. Grief for unmet needs. For misinterpretations. For younger versions of yourself who worked too hard to survive without language or support.

Reflection

1. What losses or realizations have surfaced as your understanding has shifted?

2. What younger versions of yourself are you beginning to grieve or forgive?

3. How do you allow sadness without turning it into self-blame?

Grief and self-acceptance are not opposites. They grow together.

Redefining competence

Competence is often defined narrowly: punctual, organized, socially fluent, consistent. Neurodivergent competence looks different.

Reflection

1. Where do you feel most capable, even if those strengths go unnoticed?

2. What feedback has caused you to doubt your intelligence or ability?

3. How might you define competence as alignment rather than performance?

Competence does not require masking. It requires context.

Choosing care

Understanding yourself can guide you toward neuro-affirming care and away from harmful interventions. Many dominant therapies prioritize compliance over well-being, training autistic people to appear typical at significant emotional cost.

Avoiding coercive or behaviorist interventions—including ABA (Applied Behavioral Analysis) and forced normalization—can prevent long-term harm. At its core, understanding yourself is an act of autonomy.

Diagnosis may be part of your path. It may not. What matters most is that your lived experience is treated as meaningful, credible, and worthy of care.

Reflection

1. When did you first sense that your experience differed from others'?

2. What were you hoping to find—and what were you afraid to find—when you began seeking understanding?

3. If you could speak to your past self, what would you tell them about what they already knew?

We start here because naming—whether internal or shared—is an act of relief. Sometimes, it is also an act of grief. Understanding your neurotype may not fix anything, but it can fundamentally change how you understand your own suffering—and how you protect yourself moving forward.

A reflection tool for self-understanding, support, and accommodation

The pages that follow are not a test, a declaration, or a claim that needs to be defended. They are a space to gather what you already know—about your nervous system, your patterns, your needs, and your lived experience. Many people move through life holding this information in fragments, without language or structure to make sense of it. This tool exists to help you bring those pieces into relationship with one another. You are not being asked to arrive at certainty. You are being invited to document your understanding as it exists right now, knowing that insight can deepen, shift, or change over time. Nothing here needs to be completed all at once—or at all. This is not proof. It is orientation.

Name: ________________________________

Date: ________________________________

The language I use for my neurotype (optional)

I currently describe myself as (check any that resonate):

- ☐ Autistic
- ☐ ADHD
- ☐ AuDHD
- ☐ Neurodivergent
- ☐ Questioning/Exploring
- ☐ Other: _______________

The words I use for this (in my own language):

____

How I came to understand myself

This is not a requirement. It is a record of what has helped you make meaning.

Materials or sources that have supported my understanding:

____

____

____

____

____

____

Books that have most informed my understanding:

Peer-reviewed articles or research that have informed my understanding:

Other articles or resources that have informed my understanding:

Creators, educators, or communities that have influenced my understanding:

I have found that most tools fail to capture the intersectionality of my experience:

☐ Yes   ☐ No   ☐ Sometimes / It depends

Nervous system regulation

Forms of stimming or self-regulation I most commonly use when I feel regulated:

Forms of stimming or self-regulation I most commonly use when I feel dysregulated:

____

____

____

____

____

____

____

Grounding techniques or comfort tools that tend to work for me:

____

____

____

____

____

____

My sensory profile tends to be (circle or describe):

Sensory-seeking / Sensory-avoidant / Mixed / Context-dependent

____

____

____

____

My most intense sensory aversions are:

____

____

____

____

Sensory experiences I crave or seek out:

____

____

____

____

Comfort foods / safe foods:

Ways expectations around hygiene, appearance, or "presentation" dysregulate me:

Special interests and joy

My primary special interest right now is:

Other special interests include:

____

____

____

____

____

Special interests that mattered in childhood:

____

____

____

____

____

Diagnosis, misdiagnosis, and being misunderstood

Labels or diagnoses I was given that no longer feel like the best explanation:

____

____

____

____

People or systems that misunderstood, minimized, or mislabeled me (if you want to name them):

____

____

____

____

____

____

____

____

____

____

Sense of self

Three ways I return to myself when impostor syndrome or self-doubt rise:

1. ____

2. ____

3. ____

When can I trace the feeling of "being different" back to (moment, period, or pattern)?

How does my neurotype intersect with my gender?

How does my neurotype intersect with my sexuality?

How my neurotype impacts my life (check any that apply)

☐ Socially

☐ Professionally

☐ Spiritually

☐ Executive functioning

☐ Tasks of daily living

☐ Feelings of alienation

☐ Thinking style

☐ Sensory needs

☐ How my body feels in the world

☐ Proprioception (how my body feels in space)

☐ Relationship with time

☐ Sense of direction

☐ Changes to routine

☐ Meltdowns/shutdowns

☐ Energy level

☐ Burnout

Along the spectrum of introversion to extroversion, I identify as:

____

____

____

____

____

____

____

If I had known earlier, how might my self-concept have changed growing up?

____

____

____

____

____

____

Where do I find the most neuro-affirming messaging (people, books, websites, communities)?

Has there been a single moment of recognition, or has it been an ongoing process?

How my neurotype intersects with my race/ethnicity:

____

____

____

____

____

____

____

____

How my socioeconomic background has shaped my understanding:

____

____

____

____

____

____

____

____

How my current socioeconomic reality impacts my access to support or accommodations:

Accommodations

Professional / School

Three accommodations that help me perform effectively (even informally):

1. —
2. —
3. —

Relational

What accommodations do I need around family and family time?

When I shut down or melt down, I tend to need (check any):

- ☐ Body doubling
- ☐ Space
- ☐ Quiet
- ☐ Familiar music
- ☐ Darkness
- ☐ Light

- ☐ Indoors
- ☐ Outdoors
- ☐ Near an animal
- ☐ Other:

  ____

Managing traditions

What accommodations do I need around holidays or traditions?

____

____

____

____

What needs to be true around food for me to feel okay?

____

____

____

____

How I process

My auditory processing:

My visual processing:

What this means about me as a learner:

What this means for people in conversation with me:

How I describe my processing style to enhance communication in my relationships:

Me and masking

I consider myself (circle): High-masking / Low-masking / Context-dependent

People or places that demand the most masking:

People or places that allow more unmasking:

A trait once called a "quirk" that I now understand as part of my neurotype:

I have shared this understanding with:

____

____

____

____

I may want to share this understanding with, in the future:

____

____

____

____

I want to protect this understanding from:

____

____

____

____

Me and therapy

What I need a therapist to understand about me:

How I need a therapist to be with me in session:

How metaphor impacts me in therapy:

What I need my therapist to know about eye contact:

Perception and social impact

What about neurotypical/allistic culture baffles me most:

How I feel about being photographed:

How I feel about being perceived:

____

____

____

____

My biggest fear about how I'm perceived:

____

____

____

____

What I need people to perceive about me for my self-esteem to feel intact:

____

____

____

____

Overlapping experiences

Experiences or symptoms that overlap with my neurotype:

I think these are connected to being misunderstood for a long time:

I think these would feel true about me no matter what:

Ways my neurotype has intersected with trauma:

____

____

____

____

____

Three experiences that linger most intensely:

1. ____

2. ____

3. ____

In closing, keep in mind that this document does not define you. It reflects you.

You are allowed to revise it as you revise your understanding of yourself.

Warning: There is no amount of these you *need* to identify with. You might identify with only one of the statements, you might identify with ten, or you might identify with none. This is the limitation of any list. Your identification with this list speaks to some of the small ways that being autistic shows up in your life. If you don't identify with any of it, that also speaks to the small ways that being autistic shows up in your life. Nothing about autism is monolithic.

The list, like everything else having to do with autism, is riddled with imprecision. It's merely an attempt at naming shared experiences.

You **know** you didn't **know** what to do on the playground and were always wondering where every other kid got the script.

You **know** that some people can order pizza from any restaurant, while for you, there are basically 1-2 options.

You **know** that certain clothing makes you want to jump out of your skin.

You **know** that office holiday parties are a nightmare for you.

You **know** that masking is easier if you are engaged in substance use, while sobriety can render the experience of others unbearable.

You **know** you need alone time.

You also **know** you need to connect with others on a deep and satisfying level.

You **know** that you are tuning into a level of social cues that everyone else seems oblivious to, but also missing the ones that seem to lead to popularity and being well-liked.

You **know** you replay every social interaction to try to understand where you went wrong, engaging in an endless archaeological dig.

You **know** that animals and pets bring you a calm that other people cannot.

You **know** that everything hurts you because of your high levels of sensitivity, your attunement to justice/injustice, and your inability to compartmentalize.

You **know** that things in this world are just not right.

You **know** the gender binary is a fictional concept.

You **know** that a particular smell can ruin your day.

You **know** that there are safe foods and safety clothing that allow your nervous system to find a baseline of functioning.

You **know** that you probably walk gently on this earth, so as not hurt it.

You **know** that you can see things through a prism, shifting the complexity of your perspective with each tiny turn. Other times, you can't shift at all.

You **know** that your capacity to retain information and hold memories is outside of the norm.

You **know** that there are memories you cannot retrieve because of your sensory overload at the time.

You **know** that noise-cancelling headphones are typically worth the price.

You **know** you hate surprises.

You **know** that you either have a brilliant sense of direction or no sense of direction at all.

You **know** that there is no more valid measure of autism than your lived experience.

Establishing a trusting relationship between you and that lived experience is a lifelong struggle.

Let it out, let it in

And because you **know** all these things, you **know** that it is time to give your autism the space and recognition it deserves. Whether you do that alone, with family, or in community, let your truth take up some space. Let it alter things. It is time to stop equivocating about whether you do or don't have autism and to start creating and asking for accommodations that will keep you alive.

It is time to move past deliberation (even though you will never stop deliberating) and risk the liberation and rejection that comes with unmasking.

Let your inner child print this out, let your adult self print this out, let your unmasked self create notes in the columns of it, because it's imprecise and frustrating, like most things that you try to articulate.

Let this be the end of misdiagnosis and abuse at the hands of the mental health industrial complex. Your own expertise matters. It is often all you have. Because of that, this is for you, because you **know** better than anyone what life inside your mind and body is like.

Welcome home to yourself, **your truth**, your self-preservation, your diagnosis.

What does it mean?

Self-diagnosis is rarely impulsive; it's often the result of years of thought and research. Because those of us with autistic tendencies tend to be highly cerebral, many of us have spent a long time exploring the literature, searching the internet, and filling out every self-evaluation questionnaire we could find. We've also discovered creators on social media who are speaking to us, offering a sense of understanding we didn't think was possible.

What you have done, if you've moved into the realm of self-diagnosis, is to have reclaimed your narrative. The classic narrative around autism, informed mainly by Hans Asperger in World War II Germany, is that of a white, savant-like, young boy. He saw these boys as superior to other children or adults with autism and conceptualized their autism through the lens of brilliance, eugenics, and excellence.

If you live on the fringes, this narrative does not take you into consideration. And because it doesn't represent you, your ability to claim self-knowledge about your neurotype has been hampered by exclusionary political forces that have aided your exclusion.

If you are not white, you are significantly less likely to receive a "professional" autism diagnosis. Anyone with intersecting marginalizations that exist alongside their autism is often disregarded. If you are not cisgender, your transness may be dismissed as confusion caused by autism, or your autism may be erased in favor of recognizing only your gender identity. If you are an older adult woman coming to realize you are autistic later in life, people may condescend and suggest you got the idea from TikTok. People with marginalized identities are rarely seen as part of the autistic community, or at least not the version defined and sanctioned by medical professionals.

Self-diagnosis allows for a redefinition of how autism presents itself and who is included on the spectrum. A diagnosis was never meant to confine people to the margins of a label. The use of inclusive and exclusive criteria often generates shame, fails to account for the variability of autistic expression, and ignores the reality of masking, a tool that those of us with autistic tendencies develop to cope with alienation and misalignment with social norms. Strategies that many of us have used to survive, but have kept us from being understood and believed in when we try to describe our inner world.

Self-diagnosis is a form of decolonization. Decolonization is the process by which we declare independence from a more powerful and conquering entity. In the case of autism diagnosis, the colonizing countries are the mental health industrial complex, the DSM, and the notion that expertise and lived experience are detachable. It means that expertise is a social construct created to keep those in positions of power in place, while causing those with self-knowledge to doubt themselves.

Why is it important?

Self-diagnosis is important because self-knowledge is important. The less we understand about ourselves, the harder it is to move through the world with any sense of clarity, mastery, or control. But when we claim self-knowledge as a legitimate source of truth, we become better equipped to make choices that honor who we are.

Let's take being deeply triggered by gum chewing as an example—a common experience for those with misophonia, often linked with autism. If you know your response is rooted in your nervous system and will leave you dysregulated, you're far more likely to advocate for your needs. But if you dismiss it as mere irritation, without understanding its source, you're less likely to know how to protect your well-being.

Self-diagnosis is important because you are important. And whether acknowledged or not, everyone has a neurotype. When people live in alignment with the realities of their neurotype, both its limitations and strengths, they create the possibility for fuller lives, richer creativity, and deeper community connection. Ignoring this knowledge often comes at a cost; living autistically in an allistic-dominated world—whether diagnosed or not—exacts a toll. For those diagnosed with autism, most environments aren't designed to support their ability to maintain homeostasis or self-regulate, but becoming aware of oneself can help begin to build the space needed.

The grief of recognition

Self-diagnosis, unmasking, and naming our differences can bring an avalanche of grief.

Reflection

1. What losses or realizations have surfaced since understanding yourself through a neurodivergent lens?

2. What younger versions of yourself are you mourning, or beginning to forgive?

3. How do you tend to your sadness without turning it into shame?

Grief and self-acceptance are not opposites; they grow together.

What are the benefits and limitations?

Self-diagnosis typically proves beneficial because it helps us make sense of our past experiences and understand how we got to where we are. It also becomes a guide for how we move forward, shaping future choices with newly uncovered self-knowledge. Living one's truth—much like coming out as gay—is liberating and necessary for one's overall well-being.

And while it can carry risks, the benefits usually outweigh them. The emotional and psychological toll of staying closeted or masked is often far more damaging than the vulnerability of being seen.

Self-diagnosis means betting on yourself and your self-knowledge. It's an act of courage, appointing yourself the expert of your mind and body. This requires a level of self-trust that many autistic people have been taught to suppress. This process often unfolds alongside imposter syndrome for those with marginalized identities, fueled by the lack of positive representations and recognition. Self-diagnosis is a pathway to validation, and like being autistic, it demands psychological labor to find or create places where we can protect our autistic selves with tenderness and care.

Redefining competence

Competence, as most of us learned it, is a narrow story: punctual, organized, consistent, socially fluent. But neurodivergent competence looks different.

Reflection

1. Where do you feel most capable, even if those strengths go unseen or unmeasured?

2. What kinds of feedback have made you doubt your intelligence or ability?

3. How might you redefine competence on your own terms, not as sameness, but as alignment?

Competence doesn't require masking. It requires context.

Perhaps the most valuable aspect of self-diagnosis is that it can lead us to search for neuro-affirming care, care that sees us fully, rather than reducing us to a set of symptoms to be fixed. This can look like finding a primary care provider who values neurodiversity or a therapist who rejects oppressive tools and frameworks. This means staying away from many dominant theories and interventions that claim to reduce the stress of being autistic. In reality, they often promote a coached homogenization, training us to appear typical at the expense of authenticity.

Self-diagnosis can also help us—and our loved ones—steer clear of the most harmful interventions imposed on autistic people. Dodging the world of ABA (Applied Behavioral Analysis), forced feeding programs, or coercive forms of speech and occupational therapy can mean avoiding deep and lasting trauma marked as "treatment." At its core, self-diagnosis is an act of autonomy, something often stripped from those of us with autistic tendencies as we're pushed toward assimilation and masking. Self-diagnosis is rooted in multiple versions of the truth. It says: yes, traditional assessments and medical professionals can offer insight, but lived experience is the most powerful measure. Understanding the past becomes the most impactful way to shape the future you want to create for yourself.

Reflection

Now let's explore...

1. When did you first start to wonder that something about your experience might be different from others'?

2. What were you hoping to find when you started seeking answers, and what were you afraid you might find?

3. If you could speak to your past self before you knew the words neurodivergent or autistic, what would you tell them about what they already knew?

We start here because naming is an act of relief and justice. Sometimes, it's also an act of grief. For many of us, understanding our neurotype doesn't "fix" anything, but it changes the way we understand the patterns of our own suffering.

Autism is deeply intertwined with the nervous system—not as a disorder housed inside the body, but as a neurotype that shapes how the body receives, processes, and recovers from experience.

For many autistic people, the world arrives "louder." Smells can be intense. Temperature shifts can be destabilizing. A bright room can drain us faster than we can explain. It often takes more time to recalibrate after being dysregulated by stimuli. Autistic people are frequently described as rigid or ritualistic, but rigidity is often a misunderstanding of something more human: self-preservation. Much of what looks like inflexibility is an ongoing effort to feel okay—to maintain homeostasis in environments that are rarely built for our wiring.

Before we go further, it matters to say this plainly: the most disruptive part of autistic life is often not autism itself, but the chronic mismatch between an autistic nervous system and the demands of neuro-normative spaces.

How autism relates to the nervous system

Autism is associated with differences in how the brain and nervous system process information, sensory input, and stress. Research suggests differences in brain connectivity and nervous system functioning across autistic populations, but these differences do not point to one single "autistic brain." They point to variability—different patterns of regulation, attention, and processing that can be hard to verbalize in the moment.

You may recognize this in the body before you can name it: the sudden urge to leave a room, a flooding feeling that arrives without language, the sense that your system has exceeded capacity before you can explain why. The nervous system moves faster than our own cognitions and narratives.

Autism is also highly heritable. Many autistic people come from autistic families, even if no one named it that way. When one person begins to understand themselves through a neurodivergent lens, they often become the "identified one" within a family system that may carry generations of dysregulation, masking, and unmet needs. Sometimes the first person to name what is happening feels like a canary in a coal mine—trying to give language to family patterns while being systematically ignored.

Relationships as regulation

Relationships are often discussed as something autistic people struggle with, but that framing misses something essential. For many of us, relationships can be deeply regulating—not because they are easy or intuitive, but because they offer rhythm, predictability, and shared meaning.

A relationship that feels safe can act like an external nervous system: a place where co-regulation happens through presence, attunement, and being known without explanation. This doesn't require constant closeness or emotional intensity. It often looks quieter than that—parallel presence, familiar routines, shared silences, or the relief of not having to translate ourselves.

For autistic people, regulation through relationships is not about being soothed out of our differences or shaped into something more palatable. It's about being met as we are. When a relationship allows for sensory needs, direct communication, pacing, and autonomy, it can create stability rather than demand performance. Over time, these kinds of relationships can help the nervous system settle—not because the world becomes less overwhelming, but because we are no longer alone inside of it.

Reflection

1. In your closest relationships, what signals tell you that you are safe to be yourself?

2. What kinds of interactions or expectations tend to leave you feeling dysregulated or drained?

3. How do you know when you're masking emotionally: pretending calm, pretending closeness, pretending not to care?

Relationships are often where we experience both our deepest wounds and our greatest healing.

Processing

"Processing styles" refers to the varied ways we perceive, interpret, and respond to information. Processing is cognitive, sensory, and emotional—and it shapes how we function in relationships, school, work, and daily life.

Below are a few common areas of processing difference. You do not need to relate to all of them.

Sensory processing

Autistic people can be hypersensitive (needing less sensory input) or hyposensitive (needing more sensory input), and many fluctuate depending on stress, fatigue, and context. For many autistic people, the nervous system leads, more than mood or cognition. This is why some conventional therapeutic tools can feel mismatched: it's not that autistic people don't have feelings; it's that feelings are often mediated through sensory load, pacing, and capacity.

Proprioception

Proprioception is body awareness—knowing where your body is in space. Many autistic people experience differences here: uncertainty about distance, where to stand, how much force to use, or how close is "appropriate." For some, explicit rules can feel relieving rather than restrictive.

Visual-spatial processing

Some autistic people excel at visual pattern recognition, noticing texture and complexity that others miss.

Auditory processing

Some autistic people remember spoken information almost verbatim. Others struggle to understand speech in noisy environments. Either way, volume matters. Asking for an adjustment can be one of the most challenging acts of self-advocacy.

Cognitive processing

Some autistic thinkers are highly analytic; others are more systems-oriented or holistic. Processing speed varies—some people process quickly and feel bored waiting; others need time to integrate.

Emotional processing and alexithymia

Some autistic people experience alexithymia: difficulty identifying, naming, or describing emotions in conventional language. This can look like being "disconnected from feelings," but it often reflects a different pathway between sensation, cognition, and emotion rather than a lack of emotional life.

Social processing

Many autistic people struggle with social systems rooted in hierarchy, performativity, and unspoken rules. "Not getting it" is sometimes less a deficit and more a refusal of incoherence—a wise nervous system that doesn't automatically submit to fiction.

Top-down and bottom-up processing

Some autistic people rely heavily on top-down processing: using pattern memory, context, and prior knowledge to interpret the present. Others rely more on bottom-up processing: focusing on raw sensory data first. Most people use both. There is no correct style, only the question of fit.

Reflection

What processing styles do you notice in your daily life? Do they match how you tend to move through the world?

Integration

Integration doesn't mean returning to the old way of living with a new vocabulary. It means letting new awareness change how you move through the world.

Integrating autism into one's sense of self is rarely a simple moment of recognition. It is often a slow, uneven process marked by resistance, confusion, and grief. Many autistic people come to this understanding after years—sometimes decades—of explaining themselves through other language: anxiety, sensitivity, burnout, failure. To name autism can feel destabilizing, not because it is untrue, but because it reorganizes the past.

There is also the struggle of contending with what autism has been taught to mean. For many, the word carries echoes of deficit or limitation. Integrating autism requires disentangling lived experience from inherited narratives: noticing where shame took root, where we internalized neurotypical expectations, where we learned to measure ourselves by standards never designed for us.

And yet, integration matters. Without it, autism stays external—an explanation applied after the fact rather than a truth allowed to shape life. With integration, choices become grounded rather than compensatory: rest without justification, environments that fit, relationships that do not require constant translation. Integration is not linear. It is a practice of returning.

1. What patterns do you now see with clearer eyes?

2. What relationships or environments might need to shift for your well-being?

3. How will you remind yourself of these truths when the world pressures you to forget them?

Stimming

"Stimming" (self-stimulatory behavior) refers to repetitive movements or actions used for regulation. Stimming can help manage sensory input, reduce anxiety, discharge overwhelm, and express joy. It is not inherently harmful. For many autistic people, it is protective and stabilizing.

Historically, many interventions attempted to eliminate stimming—training children to stop self-regulating in exchange for approval, compliance, or attachment. The result is often not "improvement," but internalization: distress turned inward, regulation denied, shame increased.

Some common stimming behaviors include:

- Tapping fingers or objects
- Rocking or swaying
- Humming or repeating words/phrases
- Pacing, jumping, spinning
- Focusing on small, rhythmic movements

Stimming is often the body's way of creating predictability when the environment feels chaotic. In a world that demands constant adaptation, rhythmic motion can restore a sense of control.

You have autonomy. You get to decide what regulation looks like for you.

Sensory sensitivity

Sensory sensitivity describes how some nervous systems respond intensely to sensory input. It can involve any sense—sight, sound, smell, taste, touch—and it can shift over time.

Sensory sensitivity is not a flaw in perception. It is a difference in processing. When sensory needs go unmet, the body adapts through tension, withdrawal, irritability, dissociation, or exhaustion. These are not overreactions; they are signals.

Hypersensitivity: input feels too intense (sound, light, texture, smell).

Hyposensitivity: input feels too faint; the system seeks more stimulation.

Many people are both, depending on context.

Food and safe foods

"Safe foods" are foods that feel tolerable and predictable—texture, temperature, smell, and timing already known. There are no surprises hidden inside. The body recognizes the experience. Eating becomes possible without bracing.

Safe foods are often misunderstood as rigid habits to correct. In reality, they are regulations. They allow nourishment without activation—fuel without cost—especially when the nervous system is already carrying too much.

Honoring safe foods is not about narrowing life. It is about making enough room to stay in it.

Temperature

Temperature is not background for many autistic people; it is a full-body condition. Heat can press in and make thinking feel impossible. Cold can sharpen discomfort and pull attention away from everything else. Even small shifts can reorganize capacity.

Naming temperature sensitivity matters because regulation sometimes begins not with insight, but with layers, shade, a fan, a warm drink, or permission to change the environment.

Noise

Noise often leaves a lasting imprint: braced muscles, looping thoughts, shallow sleep, a nervous system still on alert long after the room empties. Noise also accumulates. One loud moment might be tolerable. Several in a row can erode capacity for days.

Silence, here, is not avoidance. It is repair.

Light

Light can be invasive for an autistic nervous system. Fluorescent flicker, harsh brightness, screen glare—these inputs can drain capacity and contribute to headaches, irritability, shutdown, or disconnection.

Attending to light is not comfort-seeking. It is nervous system preservation.

Meltdowns, shutdowns, and burnout

Meltdowns are intense, involuntary responses to overwhelm. They are not anger, defiance, manipulation, or will. They occur when the nervous system exceeds capacity—often after cumulative sensory and emotional load. During a meltdown, the system is not accessible to reasoning. What helps is safety, reduced input, and care.

Shutdowns turn inward. Speech may drop away. Thinking slows. Engagement becomes minimal. Shutdown is often misunderstood as calm or compliance, but it is a protective narrowing of function.

Burnout is cumulative. It develops over time when recovery is repeatedly delayed or denied—often through sustained masking, chronic overload, and demands that exceed capacity. Burnout affects availability to life itself.

Each requires different care:

- Meltdowns need immediate safety and regulation
- Shutdowns need gentleness and reduced demand
- Burnout needs extended rest, environmental change, and realignment

Rest isn't avoidance. It's strategy.

Executive functioning is often framed as a moral measure: organized people succeed; disorganized people fail. But functioning is not only cognitive. It is environmental, relational, sensory, and emotional.

For many autistic people, "executive dysfunction" reflects a mismatch: unclear expectations, constant switching, sensory overload, emotional labor, and masking. In those conditions, the system stalls, not because it is broken, but because it is protecting itself.

Instead of "Why can't I just do this?" try: **"What conditions would make this possible?"**

Sensory truths

Before there were words, there were sensations. For many autistic people, early experiences of overwhelm or safety were sensory: the brightness of a light, the hum of a refrigerator, the texture of a tag. The body learned first—what to brace against, what to seek, what to avoid.

Honoring sensory truths means taking your experience seriously, even when it's hard to explain. It means building a life that responds to what the body has been communicating all along.

Reflection

1. What environments bring you a felt sense of peace or clarity?

2. When do you notice your body tensing or shutting down?

3. What minor adjustments (sound, light, temperature, texture) help you return to yourself?

Learning your sensory profile isn't indulgent. It's foundational. When we build lives that honor these truths, we replace self-criticism with attunement.

Reflection

1. What messages have you absorbed about rest, laziness, or doing nothing?

2. How do you know when your body or brain is begging for pause?

3. What forms of rest—sensory, relational, intellectual—actually restore you?

Honoring your exhaustion doesn't make you weak. It makes you trustworthy to yourself.

You've done something courageous by meeting yourself here. This workbook was never about diagnosis alone; it has always been about returning to your own authority. As you move forward, keep what resonates and release what doesn't. You are the curator of your own care.

May this process be a soft rebellion against every place that asked you to be smaller. May it be an invitation to inhabit your whole, complex, radiant self.

Executive functioning

Executive functioning is often described as a set of skills, including planning, organizing, initiating tasks, and managing time. But for many neurodivergent people, executive functioning isn't simply a cognitive capacity. It is a context-dependent state. It shifts based on sensory load, stress, sleep, hunger, emotional demand, relational safety, and how much you've been asking yourself to override your own signals.

In other words, when executive functioning drops, it may not mean you are unmotivated. It may mean your system is overloaded.

Many people have internalized a moral story about productivity: that ease equals virtue, and struggle equals failure. But neurodivergent functioning doesn't reliably respond to pressure or shame. It responds to conditions—clarity, pacing, predictability, support, and meaning.

Sometimes what looks like procrastination is actually:

- Difficulty initiating when steps are unclear
- Task-switching fatigue
- Decision overload
- Sensory overwhelm
- The nervous system protecting itself from demand

When we interpret these patterns as laziness, we miss the actual message. The question is rarely, "Why can't I do this?" The question is often, "What would make this possible?"

Reflection

1. What tasks feel easy or natural to you—and which feel inexplicably hard, even when you care deeply?

2. What kinds of environments help you start, focus, or follow through? What kinds of environments make it worse?

3. What happens inside you right before you freeze, avoid, or shut down around a task?

4. If your executive functioning is communication, what might it be trying to tell you?

Executive functioning is not a measure of your worth. It is data about your capacity.

Executive functioning is not a personal failing. It is not a measure of character, intelligence, or effort. For many neurodivergent people, it has been misunderstood, moralized, and weaponized by schools, workplaces, families, and eventually, by ourselves.

Over time, many of us learn to equate difficulty with deficiency. If a task feels heavy, we assume we are broken. If starting feels impossible, we tell ourselves we are lazy. If follow-through collapses, we shame ourselves into trying harder. But executive functioning does not respond to shame. It contracts under pressure and softens under safety.

For autistic and otherwise neurodivergent people, executive functioning often fluctuates not because of a lack of will, but because of cumulative load. Sensory input, emotional labor, masking, decision-making, and relational demand all draw from the same reservoir. When that reservoir runs low, the system does not fail—it protects. What looks like avoidance may be the nervous system saying, *there is not enough left right now.*

Many people are taught to override this message. To push. To perform. To keep going at the cost of coherence. Over time, this creates a split: one part of the self pushing forward, another pulling back. Exhaustion becomes chronic. Self-trust erodes. The body learns that it will not be listened to.

Reframing executive functioning invites a different posture—one of curiosity rather than judgment. Instead of asking, "Why can't I just do this?" We might ask, "What is making this hard right now?" Or even more gently, "What would help me feel safer approaching this?"

These questions honor the intelligence of the nervous system, rather than trying to overpower it.

It is also worth re-naming the grief here. Many neurodivergent people mourn the version of themselves they were told they should be—the organized one, the consistent one, the person who could just "get it together" if they tried. Letting go of that fantasy can feel like a loss, even as it opens space for relief. Self-compassion does not erase ambition or care; it simply removes cruelty from the process.

When executive functioning is understood as context-dependent, something softens. Difficulty no longer automatically signals failure. Rest becomes information, not indulgence. Pauses are not setbacks, but recalibrations. The goal shifts from forcing productivity to cultivating conditions that make engagement possible again.

You are not defective for needing more time, more space, more clarity, or more support. You are responding to the world with the nervous system you have. Learning to listen to that response—without immediately correcting it—can be an act of repair.

1. When executive functioning falters, what is your first story about yourself?

2. Where did you learn that story, and who benefited from you believing it?

3. What would it feel like to treat difficulty as information rather than evidence?

4. How might your relationship with effort change if you trusted your capacity instead of policing it?

There is no urgency here. Understanding your executive functioning is not another task to complete. It is an invitation to notice, to soften, and to begin again without punishment.

On Shame and Possibility

Shame has a way of slowing everything down.

It contracts the nervous system, narrows perception, and turns curiosity into self-surveillance. When shame is present, movement becomes risky. Decision-making feels heavy. Even rest can feel undeserved. For many neurodivergent people, shame is not an internal flaw—it is something learned over time, shaped by repeated experiences of being misunderstood, corrected, or asked to become more palatable.

Living inside shame creates paralysis. Not because we lack capacity, but because so much energy is spent managing how we are perceived. Executive functioning falters. Self-trust erodes. The body learns that action invites exposure, and exposure invites harm.

Moving away from shame does not magically restore ease or erase difficulty. But it does create possibility.

This kind of possibility does not always look the way neurotypical culture imagines it should. It may not be linear, ambitious, or easily measured. It may not involve productivity, visibility, or progress that can be explained to others. Sometimes possibility looks like choosing rest without justification. Sometimes it looks like asking for support instead of pushing through. Sometimes it looks like saying no, shrinking the field of expectation, or letting go of versions of success that were never designed to include you.

Possibility, here, is not about becoming more efficient or more functional. It is about becoming more aligned. It is the quiet opening that occurs when the nervous system no longer has to defend itself. It is the return of choice—when movement is no longer driven by fear or self-correction, but by a sense of internal permission.

This workbook was not created to move you toward a fixed identity or a final understanding, but to help you loosen shame's grip on your story and to remind you that your way of being has always made sense in context. If something here brought clarity, keep it. If something felt heavy or irrelevant, you are allowed to leave it behind.

Living without shame does not mean living without struggle. But it does mean that struggle no longer has to be faced alone, hidden, or explained away. From that place, possibility—your version of it—can begin to take shape.

Glossary of Terms

Ableism

Discrimination, prejudice, or harm directed toward disabled and neurodivergent people, often rooted in the assumption that neurotypical bodies, minds, and ways of functioning are inherently superior or more valuable.

Accommodations

Adjustments or modifications that are made in environments such as school, work, healthcare, or home life to support neurodivergent needs. Accommodations are not advantages; they are access.

ADHD (Attention-Deficit/Hyperactivity Disorder)

A neurodevelopmental neurotype associated with differences in attention, impulse regulation, energy, and executive functioning. ADHD can include both challenges and strengths, and it often intersects with creativity, hyperfocus, and pattern recognition.

Allistic

A term used to describe people who are not autistic. It is often used to distinguish between autistic and non-autistic (allistic) neurotypes without implying superiority or deficiency.

Autism

A neurodevelopmental neurotype characterized by differences in sensory processing, communication, nervous system regulation, and perception. Autism is often described as a spectrum due to the wide variability in lived experience. In this workbook, autism is not framed as a disorder, but as a valid and meaningful way of being.

Dyslexia

A learning difference that primarily affects reading, spelling, and language processing. Dyslexia is associated with differences in how the brain processes written language and is often accompanied by strengths in pattern recognition, spatial reasoning, and creative thinking.

Empathy

The capacity to understand, feel into, or respond to the emotional states of others. Empathy may be expressed differently across neurotypes. Autistic people often experience profound emotional empathy, though it may not always be expressed in neurotypical ways.

Executive Functioning

A set of processes related to initiating, organizing, sustaining, and completing tasks, as well as regulating attention, emotions, and energy. Executive functioning is highly context-dependent and influenced by sensory load, stress, safety, and support—not character or motivation.

Inclusion

The practice of creating environments where people of all neurotypes can participate fully, without pressure to mask, assimilate, or perform neurotypical norms.

Meltdown

An involuntary nervous system response to overwhelm. Meltdowns are not tantrums or acts of defiance; they occur when sensory, emotional, or cognitive load exceeds capacity.

Neurodevelopmental Conditions

A broad category describing neurotypes that involve differences in brain development and processing, including autism, ADHD, dyslexia, and others. This term is often used clinically, though it can carry medicalized implications.

Neurodivergent

A term describing individuals whose neurological functioning diverges from dominant societal norms. This can include autism, ADHD, dyslexia, and other neurotypes.

Neurodiversity

The understanding that neurological differences are natural variations of the human brain and should be recognized, respected, and valued as part of human diversity.

Neurodiversity Movement

A social and civil rights movement advocating for the acceptance, inclusion, and self-determination of neurodivergent people.

Neurodiversity Paradigm

An approach that emphasizes understanding neurological differences through a strengths-based, contextual, and justice-oriented lens rather than a deficit-based one.

Neuroplasticity

The brain's capacity to change and adapt over time by forming new neural connections. Neuroplasticity allows for learning, recovery, and growth throughout the lifespan.

Neurotypical

A term describing individuals whose neurological functioning aligns with dominant societal expectations and norms.

Sensory Processing Differences

Variations in how the nervous system receives, interprets, and responds to sensory input. Sensory differences may involve hypersensitivity, hyposensitivity, or fluctuation depending on context.

Shutdown

A protective nervous system response to overwhelm in which an individual may withdraw, reduce communication, or disengage to conserve energy and recover.

Special Interests

Intense, focused areas of interest that can bring joy, meaning, regulation, and expertise. Special interests are often central to identity and well-being.

Stimming

Short for self-stimulatory behavior. Stimming includes repetitive movements, sounds, or actions used to regulate the nervous system, express emotion, or maintain focus.

Language around neurodiversity continues to evolve. This glossary reflects current community-informed usage and is offered as a shared reference point, not a fixed authority.

Works Cited

Broderick, A. A., & Roscigno, R. (2021). *Autism, Inc.: The Autism Industrial Complex*. ScienceDirect.

Bollas, C. (2018). *The Shadow of the Object: Psychoanalysis of the Unthought Known*. Routledge.

McGuire, Anne. (2016). War on Autism: On the Cultural Logic of Normative Violence. Ann Arbor: University of Michigan Press.

Miller, D., Rees, J., & Pearson, A. (2021). "Masking is life": Experiences of masking in autistic and nonautistic adults. *Autism in Adulthood, 3*(4), 330–338. https://doi.org/10.1089/aut.2020.0083

Price, D. (2022). *Unmasking Autism: Discovering the New Faces of Neurodiversity*. Harmony Books.

Silberman, S. (2016). *NeuroTribes: The Legacy of Autism and the Future of Neurodiversity*. Avery / Penguin Random House.

Author Bio

Dr. Danna Bodenheimer, LCSW—known online as Dr. Danna B—is the founder of Walnut Psychotherapy Center in Philadelphia. She is a psychotherapist, educator, and writer dedicated to creating queer and neurodivergent-affirming spaces.

Across her clinical work, teaching, and writing, she explores the intersection of trauma, identity, and belonging, helping both clients and clinicians locate safety within themselves and in relationship. Her work is grounded in a compassionate, anti-pathologizing framework that blends lived experience with clinical insight.

She is the author of *Real World Clinical Social Work and On Clinical Social Work: Meditations and Truths From the Field* and the forthcoming *The Well-Attuned Therapist*. Her writing invites curiosity over certainty, permission over performance, and truth over compliance.